The Emerald Tablet of Hermes

Multiple Translations

Table of Contents

The Emerald Tablet of Hermes

Multiple Translations

Kessinger Publishing reprints thousands of hard−to−find books!

Visit us at http://www.kessinger.net

History of the Tablet

History of the Tablet (largely summarised from Needham 1980, Holmyard 1957)

The Emerald Tablet of Hermes

The Tablet probably first appeared in the West in editions of the psuedo–Aristotlean Secretum Secretorum which was actually a translation of the Kitab Sirr al–Asar, a book of advice to kings which was translated into latin by Johannes Hispalensis c. 1140 and by Philip of Tripoli c.1243.

Other translations of the Tablet may have been made during the same period by Plato of Tivoli and Hugh of Santalla, perhaps from different sources.

The date of the Kitab Sirr al–Asar is uncertain, though c.800 has been suggested and it is not clear when the tablet became part of this work.

Holmyard was the first to find another early arabic version (Ruska found a 12th centruy recension claiming to have been dictated by Sergius of Nablus) in the Kitab Ustuqus al–Uss al–Thani (Second Book of the Elements of Foundation) attributed to Jabir. Shortly after Ruska found another version appended to the Kitab Sirr al–Khaliqa wa San`at al–Tabi`a (Book of the Secret of Creation and the Art of Nature), which is also known as the Kitab Balaniyus al–Hakim fi'l–`Ilal (book of Balinas the wise on the Causes). It has been proposed that this book was written may have been written as early as 650, and was definitely finished by the Caliphate of al–Ma'mun (813–33).

Scholars have seen similarities between this book and the Syriac Book of Treasures written by Job of Odessa (9th century) and more interestingly the Greek writings of the bishop Nemesius of Emesa in Syria from the mid fourth century. However though this suggests a possible Syriac source, non of these writings contain the tablet.

Balinas is usually identified with Apollonius of Tyna, but there is little evidence to connect him with the Kitab Balabiyus, and even if there was,the story implies that Balinas found the tablet rather than wrote it, and the recent discoveries of the dead sea scrolls and the nag hamamdi texts suggest that hiding texts in caves is not impossible, even if we did not have the pyramids before us.

Ruska has suggested an origin further east, and Needham has proposed an origin in China.

Holmyard, Davis and Anon all consider that this Tablet may be one of the earliest of all alchemical works we have that survives.

The Emerald Tablet of Hermes

It should be remarked that apparantly the Greeks and Egyptians used the termtranslated as `emerald' for emeralds, green granites, "and perhaps green jasper". In medieval times the emerald table of the Gothic kings of Spain, and the Sacro catino– a dish said to have belonged to the Queen of Sheba, to have been used at the last supper, and to be made of emerald, were made of green glass [Steele and Singer: 488].

Translations From Jabir ibn Hayyan.

0) Balinas mentions the engraving on the table in the hand of Hermes, which says:

1) Truth! Certainty! That in which there is no doubt!

2) That which is above is from that which is below, and that which is below is from that which is above, working the miracles of one.

3) As all things were from one.

4) Its father is the Sun and its mother the Moon.

5) The Earth carried it in her belly, and the Wind nourished it in her belly, 7) as Earth which shall become Fire.

7a) Feed the Earth from that which is subtle, with the greatest power.

8) It ascends from the earth to the heaven and becomes ruler over that which is above and that which is below.

14) And I have already explained the meaning of the whole of this in two of these books of mine.

[Holmyard 1923: 562.]

The Emerald Tablet of Hermes

Another Arabic Version (from the German of Ruska, translated by 'Anonymous').

0) Here is that which the priest Sagijus of Nabulus has dictated concerning the entrance of Balinas into the hidden chamber... After my entrance into the chamber, where the talisman was set up, I came up to an old man sitting on a golden throne, who was holding an emerald table in one hand.

And behold the following—in Syriac, the primordial language– was written thereon:

1) Here (is) a true explanation, concerning which there can be no doubt.

2) It attests: The above from the below, and the below from the above –the work of the miracle of the One.

3) And things have been from this primal substance through a single act. How wonderful is this work! It is the main (principle) of the world and is its maintainer.

4) Its father is the sun and its mother the moon; the

5) wind has borne it in its body, and the earth has nourished it.

6) the father of talismen and the protector of miracles

6a) whose powers are perfect, and whose lights are confirmed (?),

7) a fire that becomes earth.

7a) Separate the earth from the fire, so you will attain the subtle as more inherent than the gross, with care and sagacity.

8) It rises from earth to heaven, so as to draw the lights of the heights to itself, and descends to the earth; thus within it are the forces of the above and the below;

9) because the light of lights within it, thus does the darkness flee before it.

The Emerald Tablet of Hermes

10) The force of forces, which overcomes every subtle thing and penetrates into everything gross.

11) The structure of the microcosm is in accordance with the structure of the macrocosm.

12) And accordingly proceed the knowledgeable.

13) And to this aspired Hermes, who was threefold graced with wisdom.

14) And this is his last book, which he concealed in the chamber.

[Anon 1985: 24–5]

Twelfth Century Latin

0) When I entered into the cave, I received the tablet zaradi, which was inscribed, from between the hands of Hermes, in which I discovered these words:

1) True, without falsehood, certain, most certain.

2) What is above is like what is below, and what is below is like that which is above. To make the miracle of the one thing.

3) And as all things were made from contemplation of one, so all things were born from one adaptation.

4) Its father is the Sun, its mother is the Moon.

5) The wind carried it in its womb, the earth breast fed it.

6) It is the father of all 'works of wonder' (Telesmi) in the world.

6a) Its power is complete (integra).

7) If cast to (turned towards– versa fuerit) earth,

5

7a) it will separate earth from fire, the subtile from the gross.

8) With great capacity it ascends from earth to heaven. Again it descends to earth, and takes back the power of the above and the below.

9) Thus you will receive the glory of the distinctiveness of the world. All obscurity will flee from you.

10) This is the whole most strong strength of all strength, for it overcomes all subtle things, and penetrates all solid things.

11a) Thus was the world created.

12) From this comes marvelous adaptions of which this is the proceedure.

13) Therefore I am called Hermes, because I have three parts of the wisdom of the whole world.

14) And complete is what I had to say about the work of the Sun, from the book of Galieni Alfachimi.

[From Latin in Steele and Singer 1928: 492.]

Translation from Aurelium Occultae Philosophorum..Georgio Beato

1) This is true and remote from all cover of falsehood

2) Whatever is below is similar to that which is above. Through this the marvels of the work of one thing are procured and perfected.

3) Also, as all things are made from one, by the condsideration of one, so all things were made from this one, by conjunction.

4) The father of it is the sun, the mother the moon.

5) The wind bore it in the womb. Its nurse is the earth, the mother of all perfection.

6a)Its power is perfected.

7) If it is turned into earth,

7a) separate the earth from the fire, the subtle and thin from the crude and course, prudently, with modesty and wisdom.

8) This ascends from the earth into the sky and again descends from the sky to the earth, and receives the power and efficacy of things above and of things below.

9) By this means you will acquire the glory of the whole world, and so you will drive away all shadows and blindness.

10) For this by its fortitude snatches the palm from all other fortitude and power. For it is able to penetrate and subdue everything subtle and everything crude and hard.

11a) By this means the world was founded

12) and hence the marvelous cojunctions of it and admirable effects, since this is the way by which these marvels may be brought about.

13) And because of this they have called me Hermes Tristmegistus since I have the three parts of the wisdom and Philsosphy of the whole universe.

14) My speech is finished which I have spoken concerning the solar work [Davis 1926: 874.]

Translation of Issac Newton c. 1680.

1) Tis true without lying, certain most true.

2) That wch is below is like that wch is above that wch is above is like yt wch is below to do ye miracles of one only thing.

The Emerald Tablet of Hermes

3) And as all things have been arose from one by ye mediation of one: so all things have their birth from this one thing by adaptation.

4) The Sun is its father, the moon its mother,

5) the wind hath carried it in its belly, the earth its nourse.

6) The father of all perfection in ye whole world is here.

7) Its force or power is entire if it be converted into earth.

7a) Seperate thou ye earth from ye fire, ye subtile from the gross sweetly wth great indoustry.

8) It ascends from ye earth to ye heaven again it desends to ye earth and receives ye force of things superior inferior.

9) By this means you shall have ye glory of ye whole world thereby all obscurity shall fly from you.

10) Its force is above all force. ffor it vanquishes every subtile thing penetrates every solid thing.

11a) So was ye world created.

12) From this are do come admirable adaptaions whereof ye means (Or process) is here in this.

13) Hence I am called Hermes Trismegist, having the three parts of ye philosophy of ye whole world.

14) That wch I have said of ye operation of ye Sun is accomplished ended.

[Dobbs 1988: 183–4.]

The Emerald Tablet of Hermes

Translation from Kriegsmann (?) alledgedly from the Phoenician

1) I speak truly, not falsely, certainly and most truly

2) These things below with those above and those with these join forces again so that they produce a single thing the most wonderful of all.

3) And as the whole universe was brought forth from one by the word of one GOD, so also all things are regenerated perpetually from this one according to the disposition of Nature.

4) It has the Sun for father and the Moon for mother:

5) it is carried by the air as if in a womb, it is nursed by the earth.

6) It is the cause, this, of all perfection of all things throughout the universe.

6a) This will attain the highest perfection of powers

7) if it shall be reduced into earth

7a) Distribute here the earth and there the fire, thin out the density of this the suavest (suavissima) thing of all.

8) Ascend with the greatest sagacity of genius from the earth into the sky, and thence descend again to the earth, and recognise that the forces of things above and of things below are one,

9) so as to posses the glory of the whole world– and beyond this man of abject fate may have nothing further.

10) This thing itself presently comes forth stronger by reasons of this fortitude: it subdues all bodies surely, whether tenuous or solid, by penetrating them.

11a) And so everything whatsoever that the world contains was created.

12) Hence admirable works are accomplished which are instituted (carried out– instituuntur) according to the same mode.

13) To me therefor the name of Hermes Trismegistus has been awarded because I am discovered as the Teacher of the three parts of the wisdom of the world.

14) These then are the considerations which I have concluded ought to be written down concerning the readiest operations of the Chymic art.

[Davis 1926: 875 slightly modified.]

From Sigismund Bacstrom (allegedly translated from Chaldean).

0) The Secret Works of CHIRAM ONE in essence, but three in aspect.

1) It is true, no lie, certain and to be depended upon,

2) the superior agrees with the inferior, and the inferior agrees with the superior, to effect that one truly wonderful work.

3) As all things owe their existence to the will of the only one, so all things owe their origin to the one only thing, the most hidden by the arrangement of the only God.

4) The father of that one only thing is the sun its mother is the moon,

5) the wind carries it in its belly; but its nourse is a spirituous earth.

6) That one only thing is the father of all things in the Universe.

6a) Its power is perfect,

7) after it has been united with a spirituous earth.

7a) Separate that spirituous earth from the dense or crude by means of a gentle heat, with much attention.

8) In great measure it ascends from the earth up to heaven, and descends again, newborn, on the earth, and the superior and the inferior are increased in power.

9) By this wilt thou partake of the honours of the whole world. And Darkness will fly from thee.

10) This is the strength of all powers. With this thou wilt be able to overcome all things and transmute all what is fine and what is coarse.

11a) In this manner the world was created;

12) the arrangements to follow this road are hidden.

13) For this reason I am called Chiram Telat Mechasot, one in essence, but three in aspect. In this trinity is hidden the wisdom of the whole world.

14) It is ended now, what I have said concerning the effects of the sun. Finish of the Tabula Smaragdina.

[See Hall 1977: CLVIII,]

From Madame Blavatsky

2) What is below is like that which is above, and what is above is similar to that which is below to accomplish the wonders of the one thing.

3) As all things were produced by the mediation of one being, so all things were produced from this one by adaption.

4) Its father is the sun, its mother the moon.

6a) It is the cause of all perfection throughout the whole earth.

7) Its power is perfect if it is changed into earth.

7a) Separate the earth from the fire, the subtile from the gross, acting prudently and with judgement.

8) Ascend with the greatest sagacity from earth to heaven, and unite together the power of things inferior and superior;

9) thus you will possess the light of the whole world, and all obscurity will fly away from you.

10) This thing has more fortitude than fortitude itself, because it will overcome every subtile thing and penetrate every solid thing.

11a) By it the world was formed.

[Blavatsky 1972: 507.]

From Fulcanelli (translated from the French by Sieveking)

1) This is the truth, the whole truth and nothing but the truth:–

2) As below, so above; and as above so below. With this knowledge alone you may work miracles.

3) And since all things exist in and eminate from the ONE Who is the ultimate Cause, so all things are born after their kind from this ONE.

4) The Sun is the father, the Moon the mother;

5) the wind carried it in his belly. Earth is its nurse and its guardian.

6) It is the Father of all things,

6a) the eternal Will is contained in it.

The Emerald Tablet of Hermes

7) Here, on earth, its strength, its power remain one and undivded.

7a) Earth must be separated from fire, the subtle from the dense, gently with unremitting care.

8) It arises from the earth and descends from heaven; it gathers to itself the strength of things above and things below.

9) By means of this one thing all the glory of the world shall be yours and all obscurity flee from you.

10) It is power, strong with the strength of all power, for it will penetrate all mysteries and dispel all ignorance.

11a) By it the world was created.

12) From it are born manifold wonders, the means to achieving which are here given

13) It is for this reason that I am called Hermes Trismegistus; for I possess the three essentials of the philosophy of the universe.

14) This is is the sum total of the work of the Sun.

[Sadoul 1972: 25–6.]

From Fulcanelli, new translation

1) It is true without untruth, certain and most true:

2) that which is below is like that which is on high, and that which is on high is like that which is below; by these things are made the miracles of one thing.

3) And as all things are, and come from One, by the mediation of One, So all things are born from this unique thing by adaption.

4) The Sun is the father and the Moon the mother.

5) The wind carries it in its stomach. The earth is its nourisher and its receptacle.

6 The Father of all the Theleme of the universal world is here.

6a) Its force, or power, remains entire,

7) if it is converted into earth.

7a) You separate the earth from the fire, the subtle from the gross, gently with great industry.

8) It climbs from the earth and descends from the sky, and receives the force of things superior and things inferior.

9) You will have by this way, the glory of the world and all obscurity will flee from you.

10) It is the power strong with all power, for it will defeat every subtle thing and penetrate every solid thing

11a) In this way the world was created.

12) From it are born wonderful adaptations, of which the way here is given.

13) That is why I have been called Hermes Tristmegistus, having the three parts of the universal philosophy.

14) This, that I have called the solar Work, is complete.

[Translated from Fulcanelli 1964: 312.]

From Idres Shah

1) The truth, certainty, truest, without untruth.

The Emerald Tablet of Hermes

2)What is above is like what is below. What is below is like what is above. The miracle of unity is to be attained.

3) Everything is formed from the contemplation of unity, and all things come about from unity, by means of adaptation.

4) Its parents are the Sun and Moon.

5) It was borne by the wind and nurtured by the Earth.

6) Every wonder is from it

6a) and its power is complete.

7) Throw it upon earth,

7a) and earth will separate from fire. The impalbable separated from the palpable.

8) Through wisdom it rises slowly from the world to heaven. Then it descends to the world combining the power of the upper and the lower.

9)Thus you will have the illumination of all the world, and darkness will disappear.

10) This is the power of all strength– it overcomes that which is delicate and penetrates through solids.

11a) This was the means of the creation of the world.

12) And in the future wonderful developements will be made, and this is the way.

13) I am Hermes the Threefold Sage, so named because I hold the three elements of all wisdom.

14) And thus ends the revelation of the work of the Sun.

(Shah 1964: 198).

The Emerald Tablet of Hermes

Hypothetical Chinese Original

1) True, true, with no room for doubt, certain, worthy of all trust.

2) See, the highest comes from the lowest, and the lowest from the highest; indeed a marvelous work of the tao.

3) See how all things originated from It by a single process.

4) The father of it (the elixir) is the sun (Yang), its mother the moon (Yin).

5) The wind bore it in its belly, and the earth nourished it.

6)This is the father of wondrous works (changes and transformations), the guardian of mysteries,

6a) perfect in its powers, the animator of lights.

7) This fire will be poured upon the earth...

7a) So separate the earth from the fire, the subtle from the gross, acting prudently and with art.

8) It ascends from the earth to the heavens (and orders the lights above), then descends again to the earth; and in it is the power of the highest and the lowest.

9) Thus when you have the light of lights darkness will flee away from you.

10) With this power of powers (the elixir) you shall be able to get the mastery of every subtle thing, and be able to penetrate everything that is gross.

11a) In this way was the great world itself formed.

12) Hence thus and thus marvellous operations will be acheived.

The Emerald Tablet of Hermes

[Slightly altered from Needham 1980: 371.]

TEXTUAL REMARKS

On #3 Some Latin texts have meditatione (contemplation), others mediatione (mediation). Some texts have adaptatione (by adaptation), some have adoptionis (by adoption).

On #6 'Telesmi' is a greek word, some texts have 'thelesmi'.

On #6, 7 In some texts 'Its Power is Complete' is a separate line. In the generally accepted reading, this runs into #7 producing 'Its Power is complete if versa fuerit to earth'. Where possible this has been indicated by diving these lines in 6, 6a, 7, 7a On #7, 8 In some texts the 'Wisdom, capacity' (magno ingenio) is read as referring to #7, and hence the operation of Separation is to be carried out 'carefully', in other readings the 'wisdom' is held to refer to #8 and the product of the Separation which thus ascends with 'wisdom'.

Needham quotes Ruska to the effect that sections 3, 12 and 14 are probably late additions (op.

cit)

COMMENTARIES

On #1 Hortulanus: "... the most true Sun is procreated by art. And he says most true in the superlative degree because the Sun generated by this art exceeds all natural Sun in all of its properties, medicinal and otherwise" (Davis modified by `Linden')

On #2 Albertus Magnus: Hermes says "the powers of all things below originate in the stars and constellations of the heavens: and that all these powers are poured down into all things below by the circle called Alaur, which is, they said, the first circle of the constellations". This descent is "noble when the materials receiving these powers are more like things above in their brightness and transparency; ignoble when the materials are confused and foul, so that the heavenly power is, as it were oppressed. Therefore they say that this is the reason why precious stones more than anything else have wonderful

17

powers" (60 –61). While the "seven kinds of metals have their forms from the seven planets of the lower spheres" (168).

Hortulanus: "the stone is divided into two principle parts by the magistry, into a superior part which ascends above and into an inferior part which remains below fixed and clear. And these two parts moreover are concordant in their virtue since the inferior part is earth which is called nurse and ferment, and the superior part is the spirit which quickens the whole stone and raises it up.

Wherfore separation made, and conjunction celebrated, many miracles are effected."

Burckhardt: "This refers to the reciprocal dependence of the active and the passive... essential form cannot be manifested without passive materia.. the efficacy of the spiritual power depends on the preparedness of the human 'container' and vice versa.... 'Above' and 'below' are thus related to this one thing and complement one another in its regard".

Schumaker: "There are corresponding planes in various levels of creation, hence it is safe to draw analogies between macrocosm and microcosm, the mineral kingdom and the human, animal and vegetable kingdoms etc".

Needham: "the whole affirmation looks remarkably like the doctrine that extreme of Yang generates Yin, and vice versa".

On # Hortulanus: "our stone, which was created by God, was born and came forth from a confused mass, containing in itself all the elements– and hence our stone was born by this single miracle".

Trithemius: "Is it not true that all things flow from one thing, from the goodness of the One, and that whatever is joined to Unity cannot be diverse, but rather fructifies by means of the simplicity and adaptability of the One" "What is born from Unity? Is it not the ternary? Take note: Unity is unmixed, the binary is compounded, and the ternary is reduced to the simplicity of Unity. I, Trithemius, am not of three minds, but persist in a single integrated mind taking pleasure in the ternary, which gives birth to a marvelous offspring" (Bran)

The Emerald Tablet of Hermes

Burckhardt: "the undivided, invisible Light of the unconditioned One is refracted into multiplicity by the prism of the Spirit". As the Spirit contemplates the Unity without full comprehension "it manifests the 'many–sided' All, just as a lens transmits the light it receives as a bundle of rays".

Schumaker: As God is one, all created objects come from one thing, an undifferentiated primal matter.

On #4 Hortulanus: " As one animal naturally generates more animals similar to itself, so the Sun artificially generates Sun by the power of multiplication of...the stone.... in this artificial generation it is necessary that the Sun have a suitable receptacle, consonant with itself, for its sperm and its tincture, and this is the Luna of the philosophers"

Redgrove: Sun and Moon "probably stand for Spirit and Matter respectively, not gold and silver".

Burckhardt: Sun "is the spirit (nous), while the moon is the soul (psyche)".

Schumaker: "If the moon is associated with water, as because of its 'moisture' [as] was usual, and the sun with fire, the prima materia is understood to have been generated by fire, born of water, brought down from the sky by wind, and nourished by earth".

On #5 Albertus Magnus: by this Hermes "means the levigatio [making light weight] of the material, raising it to the properties of Air. And why he says the wind carries the material [of the stone] in its belly is that, when the material is placed in an alembic– which is a vessel made like those in which rosewater is prepared– then by evapouration it is rendered subtle and is raised towards the properties of Air... And there distills and issues from the mouth of the alembic a watery or oily liquor with all the powers of the elements" (17). In metals the moisture is not separated from the dryness, but is dissolved in it; and being so dissolved, it moves about there as if it had been swallowed by the Earth and were moving about in its bowels. And on this account Hermes said 'The mother of metal is Earth that carries it in her belly'".

Hortulanus: "It is plain that wind is air, and air is life, and life is spirit... And thus it is necessary that the wind should bear the whole stone.... [However] our stone without the ferment of the earth will never come to the effect, which ferment is called food"

19

The Emerald Tablet of Hermes

Trithemius: "the wind carries its seed in her belly".

Maier: By "the wind carried him in its belly" Hermes means " 'He, whose father is the Sun, and whose mother is the Moon, will be carried before he is born, by wind and vapour, just as a flying bird is carried by air'. From the vapours of winds, which are nothing else but wind in motion, water proceeds, when condensed, and from that water, mixed with earth, all minerals and metals arise". The substance carried by the wind is "in chemical respect.. the sulphur, which is carried in mercury". Lull says "'The stone is the fire, carried in the belly of the air'. In physical respect it is the unborn child that will soon be born". To be clearer, "'All mercury is composed of vapours, that is to say of water, which the earth raises along with it into the thin air, and of earth, which the air compels to return into watery earth or earthy water" As the elements contained within are each reduced to a watery condition, they either follow the volatile elements upward as in common mercury, or they stay below with the solid elements as in philosophical Mercury "and in the solid metals". So "Mercury is the wind which receives the sulphur... as the unripe fruit from the mothers womb, or from the ashes of the burnt mother's body and takes it to a place where it may ripen".

Ripley says "our child shall be born in the air, that is the belly of the wind" [de Jong 1969: 55– 7.] Maier (2nd Comment) on "The earth is its nurse": Food changes into the substance of the eater and is then assimilated. "This harmony dominates the whole of nature, for the like enjoys the like".

The same happens in the Work and Nature "just as is the growth of the child in the mother's womb. So also a father, a mother and a nurse have been attributed to the philosophical child... it comes into being from the twofold seed and then grows as an embryo does". As a woman must moderate her diet to avoid miscarriage, "in the same way one must set about philosophical work with moderation". The Seeds also have to be united. "Philosophers say that the one comes from the East and the other from the West and become one; what does this mean but combining in a retort, a moderate temperature and nourishment?". "One may wonder why the earth is referred to as the nurse of the philosophic child, since barreness and dryness are the main properties of the element earth". The answer is that not the element, but the whole Earth is meant. "It is the nurse of Heaven not because it resolves, washes and moistens the foetus, but because it coagulates, fastens and colours the latter and changes it into sap and blood... The Earth contains a wonderful juice which changes the nature of the one who feeds on it, as

The Emerald Tablet of Hermes

Romulus is believed to have been changed by the wolf's milk into a bellicose individual" [de Jong 1969: 63 –5.]

Burckhardt: "The wind which carries the spiritual germ in its body, is the vital breath". Vital breath is the substance of the realm between heaven and earth, it "is also Quicksilver which contains the germ of gold in a liquid state". The earth is "the body, as an inward reality".

On #6 Burckhardt: the word talisman is derived from Telesma. Talismans work by corresponding to their prototype, and by making a "'condensation', on the subtle plane, of a spiritual state. This explains the similarity between the talisman, as the bearer of an invisible influence, and the alchemical elixir, as the 'ferment' of metallic transformation".

On #7 Hortulanus: The stone is perfect and complete if it is turned into earth "that is if the soul of the stone itself.... is turned into earth, namely of the stone and is fixed so that the whole substance of the stone becomes one with its nurse, namely the earth, and the whole stone is converted to ferment"

Trithemius: it is the seed from #5 that must be cast upon the earth.

Bacstrom: "Process– First Distillation".

Burckhardt: "when the Spirit is 'embodied', the volatile becomes fixed".

Schumaker: if the prime matter is to be used it must be fixed into a substance "capable of being handled".

On #7a Hortulanus: "You will separate, that is, you will dissolve, because solution is separation of parts.."

Burkhardt: The separation "means the 'extraction' of the soul from the body".

Schumaker "Since the volatile principle is fire –or sometimes, air– stability is produced by its removal. Or, alternatively but less probably, the earth is impurity ('the gross') and a purified fire ('the subtle') is what is wanted.

The Emerald Tablet of Hermes

On #8 Albertus Magnus: In intending to teach the operations of alchemy Hermes says the stone "'ascends to heaven' when by roasting and calcination it takes on the properties of Fire; for alchemists mean by calcinatio the reduction of material to to powder by burning and roasting. And the material 'again descends from heaven to earth' when it takes on the properties of Earth by inhumatio, for inhumation revives and nourishes what was previously killed by calcination".

Hortulanus: "And now he deals with multiplication [of the stone]." "Although our stone is divided in the first operation into four parts... there are really two principle parts". The ascending, non fixed, and the earth or ferment. "It is necessary to have a large quantity of this non fixed part and to give it to the stone which has been made thoroughly clean from dirt.... until the entire stone is borne above by the virtue of the spirit"

"Afterwards it is necessary to incerate the same stone,..with the oil that was extracted in the first operation, which oil is called the water of the stone" Roast or boil by sublimation until the "entire stone descends... and remains fixed and fluent". "That which is coporeal is made spiritual by sublimation, and that which is spiritual is made corporeal by descension".

Trithemius: "When the ternary has at last returned to itself it may, by an inner disposition and great delight, ascend from the earth to heaven, thereby receiving both superior and inferior power; thus will it be made powerful and glorious in the clarity of Unity, demonstrate its ability to bring forth every number, and put to flight all obscurity".

Bacstrom: "Last Digestion". "The Azoth ascends from the Earth, from the bottom of the Glass, and redescends in Veins and drops into the Earth and by this continual circulation the Azoth is more and more subtilised, Volatilizes Sol and carries the volatilized Solar atoms along with it and thereby becomes a Solar Azoth, i.e. our third and genuine Sophic Mercury". The circulation must continue until "it ceases of itself, and the Earth has sucked it all in, when it becomes the black pitchy matter, the Toad [the substances in the alchemical retort and also the lower elements in the body of man −Hall], which denotes complete putrifaction or Death of the compound".

Read, suggests this section describes the use of a kerotakis, in which metals are suspended and subject to the action of gasses released from substances heated in the base, and from their condensation and circulation.

The Emerald Tablet of Hermes

Burckhardt: "dissolution of consciousness from all formal 'coagulations' is followed by the 'crystalisation' of the Spirit, so that active and passive are perfectly united."

Schumaker: "Separate the volatile part of the substance by vaporization but continue heating until the vapour reunites with the parent body, whereupon you will have obtained the Stone".

On # Trithemius: When the ternary has returned to Unity cleansed of all impurities "the mind understands without contradiction all the mysteries of the excellently arranged arcanum".

Bacstrom: the black matter becomes White and Red. The Red "having been carried to perfection, medicinaly and for Metals" is capable of supporting complete mental and physical health, and provides "ample means, in finitum multiplicable to be benevolent and charitable, without any dimunation of our inexhaustable resources, therefore well may it be called the Glory of the whole World". Contemplation and study of the Philosopher's Stone ("L. P.") elevates the mind to God.

"The Philosophers say with great Truth, that the L.P. either finds a good man or makes one". "By invigorating the Organs the Soul makes use of for communicating with exterior objects, the Soul must aquire greater powers, not only for conception but also for retention". If we pray and have faith "all Obscurity must vanish of course".

Burckhardt: "Thus the light of the Spirit becomes constant..[and] ignorance, deception, uncertainty, doubt and foolishness will be removed from consciousness".

On # Trithemius: The Philosopher's Stone is another name for the 'one thing', and is able to "conquer every subtile thing and to penetrate every solid". "This very noble virtue... consists of maximal fortitude, touching everything with its desirable excellence".

Bacstrom: "The L.P. does possess all the Powers concealed in Nature, not for destruction but for exhaltation and regeneration of matter, in the three Departments of Nature". "It refixes the most subtil Oxygen into its own firey Nature". The power increases "in a tenfold ratio, at every multiplication". So it can penetrate Gold and Silver, and fix mercury, Crystals and Glass Fluxes.

The Emerald Tablet of Hermes

Burckhardt: "Alchemical fixation is nevertheless more inward... Through its union with the spirit bodily consciousness itself becomes a fine and penetrating power". He quotes Jabir "The body becomes a spirit, and takes on... fineness, lightness, extensibility, coloration... The spirit...

becomes a body and aquires the latter's resistance to fire, immobility and duration. From both bodies a light substance is born , which.. precisely takes up a middle position between the two extremes".

Schumaker: The product of the distillation and reunion will "dominate less solid substances, but because of its own subtlety it will 'penetrate' and hence dominate, other solid things less pure and quasi–spiritual than itself".

On # Burckhardt: "the little world is created according to the prototype of the great world", when the human realises their original nature is the image of God.

Schumaker: "The alchemical operation is a paradigm of the creative process. We may note the sexual overtones of what has preceeded"

On #12 Burckhardt: "In the Arabic text this is: "This way is traversed by the sages".

On # Hortulanus: "He here teaches in an occult manner the things from which the stone is made." "the stone is called perfect because it has in itself the nature of minerals, ofvegetables and of animals.

For the stone is three and one, tripple and single, having four natures.... and three colours, namely black, white and red. It is also called the grain of corn because unless it shall have died, it remains itself alone. And if it shall have died... it bears much fruit when it is in conjunction..."

Newton: "on account of this art Mercurius is called thrice greatest, having three parts of the philosophy of the whole world, since he signifies the Mercury of the philosophers.... and has dominion in the mineral kingdom, the vegetable kingdom, and the animal kingdom".

The Emerald Tablet of Hermes

Bacstrom: the wisdom of the world (?) is hidden in "Chiram and its Use". Hermes "signifies a Serpent, and the Serpent used to be an Emblem of Knowledge or Wisdom."

Burckhardt: "The three parts of wisdom correspond to the three great divisions of the universe, namely, the spiritual, psychic and corporeal realms, whose symbols are heaven, air and earth".

Schumaker: "The usual explanation of Tristmegistus.. is that Hermes was the greatest philosopher, the greatest priest, and the greatest king".

General

Trithemius: "our philosophy is celestial, not worldly, in order that we may faithfuly behold, by means of a direct intuition of the mind through faith and knowledge, that principle which we call God...."

Trithemius: "Study generates knowledge; knowledge prepares love; love, similarity; similarity, communion; communion, virtue; virtue, dignity; dignity, power; and power performs the miracle".

Newton "Inferior and superior, fixed and volatile, sulphur and quicksilver have a similar nature and are one thing, like man and wife. For they differ from one another only by degree of digestion and maturity. Sulphur is mature quicksilver, and quicksilver is immature sulphur: and on account of this affinity they unite like male and female, and they act on each other, and through that action they are mutually transmuted into each other and procreate a more noble offspring to accomplish the miracles of this one thing". "And just as all things were created from one Chaos by the design of one God, so in our art all things... are born from this one thing which is our Chaos, by the design of the Artificer and the skilful adaptation of things. And the generation of this is similar to the human, truly from a father and mother".

Blavatsky: the mysterious thing "is the universal, magical agent, the astral light, which in the correlations of its forces furnishes the alkahest, the philosopher's stone, and the elixir of life.

Hermetic philosophy names it Azoth, the soul of the world, the celestial virgin, the great Magnes, etc" It appears to be that which gives organisation ("the maze of force–correlations"), and form i.e.

the perfect geometry of snowflakes.

Sherwood Taylor: "the operation of the Sun.. was carried out by a 'spirit', universal, the source of all things, having the power of perfecting them. Its virtue is integral [# 6a] (ie having the power to convert the diverse into a single substance), if it be turned into earth (ie. solidified). This conveyed that the Stone was to be a solidified pneuma. Pneuma was the link between earth and heaven, having the virtue of the celestial and subterranean regions– the power of the whole cosmos from the fixed stars to the centre of the earth. It overcomes every nature and penetrates every solid. It is the source of the whole world and so it can be the means of changing things in a wonderful way.

The three parts of the philosophy of the whole world are presumably of the celestial, terrestrial, and subterranean regions".

Shah: The table is "the same as the Sufi dictum... 'Man is the microcosm, creation the macrocosm —the unity. All comes from One. By the joining of the power of contemplation all can be attained.

This essence must be separated from the body first, then combined with the body. This is the Work. Start with yourself, end with all. Before man, beyond man, transformation'".

A COMMENTARY OF IBN UMAIL

HERMUS said the secret of everything and the life of everything is Water.... This water becomes in wheat, ferment; in the vine, wine; in the olive, olive oil.... The begining of the child is from water.... Regarding this spiritual water and the sanctified and thirsty earth, HERMUS the great, crowned with the glorious wisdom and the sublime sciences, said [#1] Truth it is, indubtible, certain and correct, [#2] that the High is from the Low and the Low is from the High. They bring about wonders through the one, just as things are produced from that one essence by a single preparation. Later by his statement [#4] Its father is the Sun and its mother the Moon he meant their male and their female. They are the two birds which are linked together in the pictures given regarding the beginning of the operation, and from them the spiritual tinctures are produced. And similarly they are at the end of the operation. Later in his statement [#7 ?] the subtle is more honourable than the gross, he means by the subtle the divine spiritual water; and by the gross the earthly body. As for his later statement [#8] with gentleness and wisdom it will ascend from the earth to the sky, and will take fire from the higher lights, he means by this the distillation and the raising of the water into the air. As for his later statement [#8a] It will descend to the earth, containing the strength of the high and the low, he means by this the breathing in (istinshaq) of the air, and the taking of the spirit from it, and its subsequent elevation to the highest degree of heat, and it is the Fire, and the low is the body, and its content of the controlling earthly power which imparts the colours. For there lie in it those higher powers, as well as the earthly powers which were submerged in it.

The natural operation and decay causes it to be manifest, and hence the strength of the earth, and of the air, and of the higher fire passed in to it. Later he said [#9] it will overcome the high and the low because it in it is found the light of lights: and consequently the darkness will flee from it. [See Stapleton et al. p 74, 81.]

APPENDIX

Translation from Roger Bacon's edition of Secretum Secretorum made c 1445

1)Trouth hath hym so, and it is no doubt,

2) that the lover is to the heigher, and the heigher to the lower aunsweren.

The worcher forsoth of all myracles is the one and sool God, of and fro Whom Cometh all meruelous operacions.

3) So all thynges were created of o soole substance, and of o soole disposicion,

4) the fader wherof is the sone, and the moone moder,

5) that brought hym forth by blast or aier in the wombe, the erthe taken fro it,

6) to whom is seid the increat fader, tresour of myracles, and yever of vertues.

7) Of fire is made erthe.

7a) Depart the erthe fro the fire, for the sotiller is worthier than the more grosse, and the thynne thynge than the thik. This most be do wisely and discretly.

8) It ascendith fro the erth into the heven, and falleth fro heven to the erthe, and therof sleith the higher and the lower vertue.

9)And yf it lordship in the lower and in the heigher, and thow shalt lordship aboue and beneth, which forsoth is the light of lightes, and therfor fro the wolle fle all derknesse.

10) The higher vertue ouer–cometh all, for sothe all thynne thyng doth in dense thynges.

11a) After the disposicion of the more world rynneth this worchyng.

13) And for this prophetisyng of the trynyte of God Hermogenes it called Triplex, trebil in philosophie, as Aristotle seith.

[See Manzalaoui 1977: 65 –6.]

Translation of same source, made c. 1485.

1) The trwthe is so, and that it is no dowght,

2) that lower thyngis to hyer thyng, and hyer to lower be correspondent. But the Werker of myraclis is on Godde alone, fro Home descendyth euiry meruulus werk.

3)And so alle thyngis be creat of one only substauns, be an only dysposicion,

4) of home the fadyr is the sonne, and the mone the modyr,

5) qwyche bar her be the wedyr in the wombe. The erthe is priuyd fro her–to.

The Emerald Tablet of Hermes

6)This is clepyd or seyd the fadyr of enchauntmentis, tresur of myracclys, the yessuer of vertuys.

7) Be a lytil it is made erthe.

7a) Depart that qwyche is erthly fro that qwyche is fi Fry, for that qwyche is sotel is mor wurthy han that qwyche is grose, and that rar, porous, or lyght, is mor bettyr than qwiche is thyk of substauns. This is done wyseli or dyscretly.

8) It ascendyth fro the erth in−to heuyn and fallyth fro heuyn in−to erth, and ther−of it sleth the ouyr vertu and the nedyr vertu, so it hath lorchyp in the lowe thyngis and hye thingis,

9) and thu lordschyppist vppeward and downward, and with the is the lyght of lyghtys. And for that alle derkness schal fle fro the.

10) The ovyr vetu ouircomyth alle, for euiry rar rhyng werkyth in to euiry thyk thyng.

11a) And aftyr the dysposicion of the mor world rennyth thys werking.

13) And for that Hermogines is clepyd threfold in filosophye, and of the meruellys of he world.

[See Manzalaoui 1977: 174−5]

BIBLIOGRAPHY

Albertus Magnus, Book of Minerals, trans D. Wyckoff, OUP, 1967.

Anon Meditations on the Tarot. Amity House, 1985 pp21−6 Brann, N.L. "George Ripley and the Abbot Trithemius", Ambix, vol 26, no 3, pp 212− 220, 1979.

Blavatsky, H.P. Isis Unveiled. Theosophical University Press, 1972. pp 507−14.

Burckhardt, T. Alchemy. Stuart and Watkins, London 1967 pp 196 −201.

The Emerald Tablet of Hermes

Davis, Tenny L. "The Emerald Tablet of Hermes Tristmegistus: Three Latin versions which were current among later Alchemists", Journal of Chemical Education, Vol.3, no.8, pp 863–75, 1926.

de Jong, H.M.E. Michael Maiers's Atlanta Fugiens: Sources of an alchemical Book of Emblems.

E.J. Brill, Leiden, 1969.

Dobbs, B.J. "Newton's Commentary on the Emerald Tablet of Hermes Trismegistus" in Merkel, I and Debus A.G. Hermeticism and the Renaissance. Folger, Washington 1988.

Fulcanelli. Les Demeures Philosophales. Jean Jacques Pavert, Paris, 1964.

Hall, M.P. The Secret Teachings of all Ages. Philosophical Research, L.A. 1977 pp CLVII –CLVIII.

Holmyard, E.J. "The Emerald Table" Nature, Oct 6th pp 525–6, 1929.

Holmyard, E.J. Alchemy, Pelican, Harmondsworth 1957. pp95–8.

Linden, Stanton J. ed. "The Mirror of Alchimy Composed by the Thrice–Famous and Learned Fryer Roger Bacon (1597), Garland, NY. 1992.

Manzalaoui, M.A. Secretum Secretorum: Nine English Versions, Early English Text Society.

OUP, 1977.

Needham, J.Science and Civilisation in China vol 5, part 4: Spagyrical discovery and invention:

Apparatus, Theories and gifts. CUP, 1980 Read, John Prelude to Chemistry, G Bell, London, 1939 pp15, 51–5 Redgrove, S. Alchemy: Ancient and Modern. William Rider, London, 1922. pp40–42.

The Emerald Tablet of Hermes

Sadoul, J. Alchemists and Gold. G.P. Putnams, N.Y. 1972 pp 25–6.

Schumaker, Wayne. The Occult Sciences in the Renaissance. University of California, Berkely 1972, pp 179–80 Shah, Idres. The Sufis. Octagon, London 1977, p 198 Sherwood Taylor, F. The Alchemists. Paladin, London, 1976, pp77– 8.

Stapleton, H.E., Lewis, G.L, Sherwood Taylor, F. "The sayings of Hermes quoted in the Ma Al–Waraqi of Ibn Umail. " Ambix, vol 3, pp 69–90, 1949.

Steele, R. and Singer, D.W. "The Emerald Table". Proceedings of the Royal Society of Medicine vol 21, 1928.

CPSIA information can be obtained
at www.ICGtesting.com
Printed in the USA
BVHW010606150720
583689BV00010B/418